Persevere

Why Giving Up is Not an Option

Stories of Empowered Women
Curated by
Dr. *Timogi*

Greetings Authors,

In the journey of life, we all face moments that test our strength, resilience, and resolve. These are the moments that shape us, define us, and ultimately, make us who we are. It is in these moments that we discover the true power of perseverance. Thank you for sharing your voice in this anthology, Persevere: Why Giving Up is Not an Option.

This book is a **celebration of women** who have faced insurmountable odds and emerged stronger. It is a tribute to the spirit of determination that resides within every woman. By sharing your story, you will inspire others to find their strength, to keep going even when the going gets tough, and to understand that giving up is never an option.

Your story matters. It has the power to touch hearts, change lives, and provide solace to those who may be struggling with their own battles. Whether you've overcome personal challenges, professional obstacles, or have simply refused to let life's setbacks define you, your experience is a beacon of hope and resilience.

In gratitude of your submission,

Foreword

When asked to write the foreword for this book, I graciously accepted, unaware that life was about to test my perseverance in ways I couldn't have imagined. The very next day was the long-anticipated "Chill and Chew Brunch." I was filled with gratitude. God had blessed me with my own event center after years of prayer, and now, my guests would see it for the first time. Emotions swirled inside me—pride, joy, awe at what God had done. The brunch was a success, and as I tidied up afterward, I whispered, "Thank you, God. You are so awesome."

On the drive home, my phone rang. It was my sister, and from the way she said my name, I knew something was terribly wrong. Our oldest brother, Ottis, had suddenly passed away.

Just thirty minutes earlier, I had been overflowing with joy; now I was overwhelmed with sorrow. How could God, in all His goodness, allow this to happen? As I sat in the passenger seat, crying uncontrollably, I grappled with the sudden shift from joy to pain.

Desperate for comfort, I forced myself to go to church, hoping the praise, worship, and sermon would break through the darkness. I found some relief, but the grief still clung to me.

Then Dr. Timogi called to touch base about, this foreword. I told her about my brother, and without hesitation, she prayed for me. Perseverance, I realized, isn't just about pushing through—it's also about being surrounded by the right people, those who show up just when you need them. God's timing is perfect. He sends reminders, often through others, that He is still with us, even in our most painful moments.

I've always lived by the Nike mantra, "Just do it." No matter how hard it seems, you are stronger, smarter, and more powerful than you think. I began reading the stories in this book, and they encouraged me deeply. Each author has faced their own trials, but their words— "The show must go on," "Speak life into your situation," "Your setbacks are not the end but the beginning"—are powerful reminders that we all have the strength to keep going.

This book is a testament to the power of perseverance. Every page is filled with stories, insights, and reflections on enduring hardship and the triumph that awaits those who refuse to give up. Whether you're on the brink of a new journey or facing challenges that feel insurmountable, this book will remind you that you *can* persevere. Even when it seems impossible, you absolutely can—and you absolutely must—because the world is waiting for your story of triumph.

No matter what you're going through, know that victory is within reach. Speak life into your situation, just do it, and keep moving forward. May this book inspire you to continue your journey with relentless determination, and may your perseverance lead you to the life and dreams you envision.

Perseverance Principles

1. Have Faith and Gratitude in Difficult Times - Holding onto faith, even in the face of deep sorrow, can provide the strength to persevere.
2. The Right Circle Provides Support - Surrounding yourself with supportive people is key. Having a strong, connected community can lift you up during challenging moments.
3. Inner Strength Mantras - Mantras can build self-belief and resilience. Have some committed to memory for life's difficult moments.

Linease D. Washington affectionately called Dr. Lin was born in Koenton, Alabama and raised in St. Petersburg Florida. She holds a Doctor of Divinity degree, is a domestic violence overcomer, and has been featured in numerous publications and media outlets and received numerous awards and accolades for her community service and philanthropy initiatives. Before she decided to walk into her Purpose, she enjoyed a successful career as a Human Resources Professional. She is the CEO, Creative Designer at ACA Event Solutions and A Cream Affair Event Center and founder of the global women's organization S.W.A.G "Successful Women Around the Globe" Linease believes every moment is a gift that should be cherished and celebrated.

www.acaeventsoultions
info@acaeventsolutions

Contents

The Show Must Go On

I was struck by a vivid vision and an overwhelming feeling that the opportune moment had arrived for me to do a one-woman show in honor of my deceased brother. The divine had spoken to me and impelled me to be open and articulate the emotions that had been brewing inside me and to convey my agony and elation through music.

On the 8th of December 2018, I reserved the Triad Theater in New York, envisioning a space that would not only be comfortable for me but inviting for my guests. Having been involved in the music industry previously, entertaining people failed to fulfil my expectations. This time around, I was determined to construct a space that resembled an intimate living area. Picturing my friends gathering for a casual impromptu musical performance with my band, I was mindful that this was my chance to: JUST BE ME and to create a show that mirrored the experiences that I was presently undergoing in my life.

With the show booked, flyers printed and posted, and social media buzzing with posts about the upcoming event, tickets were available to be purchased. Soon I would share a part of me with an audience. However, battling depression and anxiety for 24 years, self-doubt plagued me, and I began to wonder if what I had envisioned would come to pass. This disorder, my little secret that no one knew existed, robbed me of completing other dreams and aspirations.

Despite my depression and anxiety, I fought daily telling myself that this show is necessary. "You can do this girl," I said to myself. With only seven days left until showtime, sales stood at only 6 tickets. Then, the phone rings and it is a dreaded call from the theater owner. They want to help me fill this show and suggested reducing the ticket price or cancelling the show altogether. My theater contract required me to sell a minimum of 100 tickets to receive the entire proceeds from ticket sales. Each ticket also came with a two-drink minimum that went directly to the theater. Fear of failure started to take hold, but I refused to cancel my show or reduce the ticket price.

I opted to stand firm with a mustard seed of faith, knowing my gift would make room for me. I am worthy of a $45 ticket. I wouldn't budge on the ticket price. In that moment I decided not to get caught up in the details of making ticket sales, but to concentrate on the goal; honor my brother. The owner of the theater called the next day to hear my final decision. My anxiety was shouting," Cancel or reduce the ticket prices," but I remembered writing down one day, "My lack of resources will not determine my value." I began thinking about how to overcome this challenge.

I have over 1,800 numbers in my phone and over 750 email contacts. I began to make calls, send texts and emails to sell tickets. As a result, my contacts began buying tickets. My phone rang again later that day. It was the theater owner again questioning the amount of ticket sales. Audrey, he asked, "How have you sold 175 tickets in 4 hours?" That was the moment that I knew I had stood firmly in my God given gift, operating in a space of believing fully in myself. By the end of the day, six days away from the show, it was sold out! 250 tickets sold!

On the night of the event, people from as far off as Germany showed up for the event. They had stumbled on my show while visiting New York and thought it would be an excellent show. They were further amazed to know that the tickets were only $45. The quality of the show was worth so much more, they shared. Victorious over anxiety I delivered the caliber of show I envisioned, with the aid of the Almighty, who enabled me to modify my perspective, and concentrate on my objective.

Perseverance Principles

1. It is never too late to live your dreams. Start right now.

2. Don't get caught in the details, focus on the goal and commit.

3. You can still grow into who you want to be.

Audrey Givens started singing at age 6, as one of The Givens Kids starring on *What's Happening* on NBC in an iconic moment singing "Bubbling Brown Sugar." Throughout her career she's worked with greats including Stevie Wonder and Bernard Belle. Life happened and Audrey stopped singing for more than a decade until she auditioned for BET's Sunday Best Season 7, placing in the Top 20, out of 20k hopefuls renewing her purpose knowing "it's not about me it is about connecting with God, his people, and living in truth." She now travels singing at events and speaking about her industry experience to aspiring artists.

www.AudreyGivens.com

Perseverance and Potential: Daring to Dream and Defy Expectations

Imagine looking up from your schoolwork and hearing the words, "THOSE kids aren't going to college." This was the harsh message my son overheard one day as his teacher conversed with colleagues out in the hallway outside his classroom. My middle schooler rushed rush home, and in a voice filled with urgency and doubt asked, "Mom, I'm going to college, right?" His eyes searched mine for reassurance. My heart sank as I wondered, "How can it be that my son's own teacher has already written off his future?" In that moment, I knew we had a long road ahead, but I also knew we would face it together. Son, I said, "You can go to college if you want to!"

From that day forward, we began planning. I made it clear to his teacher that we would not allow him to take options off the table for my son. "Maybe he will go and maybe he won't, but it's NOT up to you," I asserted. This was a turning point, not just in our family's conversations about college, but in how we approached every challenge that came our way.

My son embraced the vision of his future and got to work. He demonstrated a resilience that was nothing short of inspiring. But this wasn't the first time someone had cast doubt on his potential.

"Your son has pervasive developmental delays. I'm very sorry," a doctor had once told us, offering little encouragement. Such a stark assessment felt like a punch in the gut. His preschool teacher affirmed this sentiment, adding, "He's ALWAYS going to be like this." It was as though they were sealing his fate before he had even had a chance to start living. To stay encouraged, I repeated this mantra, "Speak LIFE into the heart of your children – They're listening."

Refusing to accept these limitations, we sought out the help he needed. Speech therapy, occupational therapy, gymnastics – we left no stone unturned. Each session was a step forward, each small victory a testament to his determination. Our son went mainstream in middle school, tackling subjects that once seemed insurmountable. He survived Biology with the amazing Ms. Arya. Genes! Chromosomes! AND Punnett squares? You name it; he nailed it.

Even as he made strides, skepticism persisted when he approached high school. "He can go to our auto repair program!" an advisor very strongly suggested. Now, don't get me wrong- a good mechanic is a lifesaver, but my son had never expressed a desire to be a mechanic. In fact, no one at school had asked my son if that's what he wanted. Why should his dreams be confined to someone else's expectations? NO child has to be what he doesn't want to be. Especially when he's willing to work for his dreams.

Our son continued to defy the odds. He maintained a 3.5 GPA while playing football, earning high academic honors at both the state and regional levels. His hard work and dedication culminated in the arrival of four college admission letters, and he is a proud college graduate today.

As a nation, we have roughly 5,300 colleges, each one a potential launchpad for a young dreamer. Every child deserves to be taught, and treated, as if they have the potential to pursue higher education if they so desire. It's not just about going to college; it's about instilling in our children the confidence to dream big and the tenacity to make those dreams a reality.

My journey with my son has taught me invaluable lessons. When we speak light into our children, when we refuse to let others dictate their paths, and when we support their dreams, we give them space to achieve greatness on their terms. Remember, perseverance is not just about *enduring* hardships but about consciously *advancing* with urgency and intention to create the fulfilling outcomes you desire.

Perseverance Principles

1. **Believe in Your Child's Potential**: Never let others define what your child can or cannot achieve. Your advocacy and belief in them can fuel their self-confidence and determination.
2. **Speak Life and Positivity**: Words matter. Use them wisely to encourage and uplift your children. Let them know that their dreams are valid and achievable, with determination and effort.
3. **Support Their Dreams Relentlessly**: Whether through educational resources, extracurricular activities, or simply being their biggest cheerleader, unwavering parental support is crucial in helping children reach their full potential.

Carol Muleta, a Parenting Consultant, and Founder of The Parenting 411®, delivers "information parents need from sources they can trust.®" She gives working moms tools and strategies to consciously connect with their children, confidently teach them skills for life, and courageously tap into the JOY in their parenting journey. Carol reaches parents through keynotes, coaching, and The Parenting 411® Podcast. A 7x best-selling author, she has been honored as DC Mother of the Year, Radio Personality of the Year, and Presidential Lifetime Achievement Award recipient.

www.carolmuleta.com

www.theparenting411.com

Twin Strength

For over two decades, I endured an abusive marriage. I met him when I was just 16, shortly after my father passed away. Young and grieving, I clung to the idea of love without recognizing the warning signs. The first time he hit me, I was shocked and scared. But I didn't leave. I didn't know how. The destruction of my confidence, the isolation from my family, and the constant fear of his temper became my daily reality. The beatings, public humiliation, and terror were all I knew.

My husband's temper was like a storm that never cleared. I spent years walking on eggshells, afraid of the next outburst. The mental and physical abuse were relentless. My world became small. I hid my wounds—black eyes, busted lips, and the emotional scars of being terrorized. I learned to shut down mentally during his many assaults. It was how I coped. My coping mechanism allowed my survival instincts to kick in. Perseverance allowed me to push through the darkest days of pain and trauma and look forward to a brighter future.

I had an identical twin sister. She died far too soon, leaving an emptiness in my heart. We had a deep connection, a bond that only twins understand. She knew when I was hurting, sad, or feeling defeated without me having to say a word. Losing my identical twin sister was unbearable. She wasn't just my sister; she was my lifeline. We shared so much, including the joy of raising children of our own. When my sister passed away it felt like the end of my world. She was my link to the joy, safety, and unconditional love of my family, a love that I desperately needed. Through it all, my sister was there, a constant source of emotional support.

After my sister died, I had to find a way, not just for myself, but for the resilience she had helped me find. In the face of my loss, I found the strength to leave my abusive marriage. While the physical abuse stopped, the emotional scars lingered. The words I had heard so often—stupid, worthless—echoed in my mind. But somewhere deep within, I knew those words weren't true. My sister was the only one to see past it all, she knew the real me underneath the hurt and fear.

My sister's spirit became my guiding light, reminding me that I could survive anything. Her memory gave me the strength to look forward to a future filled with peace and self-love. She taught me that I can power through any heartache, and that even in the darkest moments, I can persevere. Though I miss my sister every single day, I honor her by continuing to live and love fully. The bond we shared reminds me that I am never alone.

My sister's spirit helped me to rebuild my life. I realized that while she was no longer physically here, the connection we shared was forever. She knew the emotional scars I carried, even when I hid the physical ones. She was my lifeline that helped me keep afloat when I felt I was drowning. Even in the darkest moments, I knew she wouldn't want me to give up. I fought to reclaim my life one step at a time. It gave me the courage to leave my abuser, to heal from the emotional scars, and believe in myself again.

Leaving my abusive marriage was a turning point in my life. Free from the constant fear and control, I began to heal. The physical abuse had stopped, but the emotional wounds remained. I battled feelings of worthlessness and self-doubt, because of verbal and emotional torment. My sister's love continued to be my guide. Her belief in me allowed me to believe in myself.

With time, I learned to embrace the resilience that had always been within me. I leaned into the strength that my twin had always seen in me and moved forward. I know she would be proud of how far I've come. Our bond may no longer be physical, but it remains, evident to the power of love, connection, and the unbreakable spirit of a twin.

Perseverance Principles

1. **Resilience -** The strength to survive and rebuild can be found within, fueled by love and hope.
2. **Unbreakable Bonds -** Seek your trusted relationships for unwavering support, especially in the darkest moments.
3. **Let Go to Heal -** Healing begins with rejecting harmful thoughts and reclaiming your self-worth.

Christy Owens is a sixty something retired computer programmer from Brooklyn, NY. She's a college graduate, which she achieved in her 50's after leaving her marriage. While in college she learned how to swim, of which she is enormously proud. Christy is an avid reader and loves Jackie Collins! She once wrote, (actually, typed on a typewriter) and shopped a novel back when there was no such thing as self-publishing. She is an active volunteer in her community.

The Juggle is Real: How I Conquered College and Career

At seventeen, while many of my peers were still navigating the final year of high school, I found myself on the campus of Sam Houston State University, eager but anxious about the journey ahead. Coming from a single-parent household, I was acutely aware of the financial burdens that college would place on my family. My mother and her parents had never attended, so the idea of higher education was unfamiliar territory.

I had little guidance on what to expect or how to prepare for college. During this time, I noticed that my mother was in a very strained relationship with her then husband. This situation affected our relationship deeply, creating a rift that made it difficult for us to communicate, which was always a challenge. The tension reached a point where she even refused to provide her W2's a crucial document needed for me to complete my financial aid application. This refusal was not just a bureaucratic hurdle- it reflected the growing distance between us and the challenges I had to navigate on my own.

Being on a college campus, I soon realized that my lack of support made it difficult to make ends meet. The financial pressures eventually forced me to make tough decisions. My great uncle stepped in where he could, contributing to the last year's tuition, but it quickly became clear that even his assistance wouldn't be enough to see me through the remainder of the year. After much struggle, I returned home before completing my final semester.

Returning home was one of the hardest decisions I had to make. I was determined to break generational curses. I saw those who lacked drive and ambition, who had no goals or vision for a better future. I wanted more for myself and was committed to pursuing a different path, one that would lead to growth, achievement, and breaking free from the limitations that had defined previous generations and others in my family. Leaving felt like a step backward, and I struggled with feelings of failure and disappointment.

Returning home gave me a chance to regroup and figure out my next move. I enrolled at the University of Houston Downtown and lived with a friend, Darin, I met on campus. I was determined to continue my education while also taking on full-time work. This decision marked the beginning of an incredibly demanding period in my life, but one that would ultimately shape my resilience and work ethic.

Balancing full-time work, full-time school, and did I mention, joining the police academy was a challenge unlike any I had faced before. My days started early and ended late, with little time for rest in between. I remained focused on my studies, knowing that a degree was crucial for my future. At the same time, working full-time was necessary to support myself financially. The police academy added another layer of intensity, requiring physical, financial, and mental endurance. There were days when I wondered how I would manage it all, but I knew I couldn't afford to let any aspect slip. I learned how to push through exhaustion, how to manage my time down to the minute, and how to keep my eyes on the goal, even when the journey seemed overwhelming.

Looking back, the grueling schedules I maintained were defining moments in my life. The skills I developed during this time—resilience, time management and determination—have stayed with me, guiding me through every subsequent challenge.

After graduating from the police academy in August 2004 and earning my bachelor's degree in interdisciplinary studies from the University of Houston- in December 2002, I enrolled in a master's program and graduated in May 2007 with a degree in Criminology. My journey didn't stop there. I became a Sergeant and continued to grow. In 2015, I achieved another milestone by earning a master's degree in human resources development.

Although the road was far from easy, I'm proud of how far I've come and grateful for the lessons learned along the way. My experiences have shaped me and continue to drive my pursuit of excellence. I look forward to the future with confidence, knowing the resilience and skills I've developed will support me in all my endeavors.

Perseverance Principles

1. **Time Management is Crucial** - Efficiency isn't optional; it's essential.
2. **Resilience Builds Strength** - Bounce back stronger with every challenge.
3. **Lean** - When you need help lean on others and let them lean on you.

Jamaliah Davis has over a decade of experience in law enforcement, Jamaliah has honed her expertise in crisis management, conflict resolution, and strategic team leadership. Her current focus is on human resources, where she enhances organizational culture and drives employee engagement. Her background provides a unique perspective on safety, integrity, and effective communication within the workplace. She continually expands her knowledge through advanced HR training, ensuring she remains at the forefront of best practices in the field. As a professional organizer and entrepreneur behind Clutter Away by Shae, she specializes in creating efficient, clutter-free spaces that enhance both functionality and peace of mind.

Amplify Your Value or Be Devalued

In leadership, value isn't just about worth—it's about perception, influence, and impact. For women in leadership roles, amplifying your value is a necessity. If you don't actively demonstrate and communicate your value, you risk being devalued, overlooked, and marginalized

The Double-Edged Sword of Value Perception

Women in leadership often face a double-edged sword when it comes to value perception. Society holds women to higher standards, often expecting them to prove their competence and capability repeatedly. Traditional gender biases can lead to the undervaluation of women's contributions. Women must be deliberate and proactive in showcasing their value, or risk being sidelined or underappreciated.

The Importance of Self-Advocacy

A critical aspect of amplifying your value is self-advocacy. Women have been conditioned to believe that hard work alone will be rewarded. Visibility is as important as competence. Women must articulate their achievements, skills, and contributions confidently and unapologetically.

Self-advocacy doesn't mean boasting or overshadowing others. It means owning your successes and ensuring they are acknowledged. The key is to ensure that your value is recognized by those who have the power to elevate your career.

There was a time in my career where I was told I would succeed my boss, who announced her retirement for the next year. I was extremely excited. She incrementally began to move over her tasks to me in preparation for her exit.

A year and 6 months passed, and she was still employed. By this time, I was doing my job and most of hers. I never said a word. Instead, I pursued management opportunities externally. I did not advocate for myself. I know better now.

Building and Leveraging Networks

Another powerful way to amplify your value is by building and leveraging networks. Networks are about cultivating relationships that can support, mentor, and advocate for you. Women often find themselves isolated, especially in male-dominated industries. By actively engaging with networks, you can create a support system that amplifies your voice and your value.

Embracing Continuous Learning and Adaptability

In today's world, the value of a leader is often tied to their ability to adapt, learn, and grow. For women in leadership, embracing continuous learning is essential to staying relevant and amplifying your value. This doesn't just mean acquiring new skills—it means staying informed about industry trends, understanding emerging challenges, and being open to new ways of thinking.

Continuous learning also demonstrates a commitment to personal and professional growth, which is a key aspect of leadership value. By positioning yourself as a leader who is always evolving, you enhance your own capabilities and set an example for others to follow.

The Power of Strategic Communication

Effective communication is at the heart of amplifying your value. It's not enough to simply do the work; you must also communicate your vision, goals, and achievements strategically. This involves mastering the art of storytelling and the science of data.

Storytelling allows you to connect with your audience on an emotional level, making your value memorable and impactful. Data, on the other hand, provides the concrete evidence needed to back up your claims. By combining these two elements, you can craft a compelling narrative that showcases your value in a way that resonates with others.

Strategic communication also means knowing when and how to assert your ideas and contributions. It's about finding the balance between being assertive and approachable, ensuring that your voice is heard without alienating others. This balance is crucial for women leaders, who often face scrutiny for their communication styles.

Owning Your Space and Defining Your Brand

Amplifying your value requires that you own your space and define your personal brand. As a woman in leadership, you must be clear about what you stand for, what you bring to the table, and how you want to be perceived. Your brand is how you present yourself, the value you deliver, and the impact you make.

Owning your space means not shying away from leadership opportunities, even when they push you out of your comfort zone. It means standing firm in your decisions, even in the face of opposition. By defining and owning your brand, you ensure that your value is consistently recognized and respected.

Perseverance Principles

1. In leadership, value is both a currency and a beacon. For women, amplifying that value is crucial to ensuring that their contributions are recognized, their voices heard, and their impact felt.
2. By embracing self-advocacy, leveraging networks, committing to continuous learning, mastering strategic communication, and owning their space, women leaders can not only amplify their value but also pave the way for future generations of women to do the same.
3. The choice is clear: amplify your value, or risk being devalued. You are the pilot, not the passenger of your career.

Dr. Karen Hills Pruden is the CEO of Pruden Global Business Solutions Consulting, a leadership training and professional development organization committed to strategizing with high-performing professionals. Dr. Karen is on a mission to collaborate with professionals while guiding them through her 5-Step framework to Amplify Your Value. Dr. Karen has worked in leadership in the tax industry, local government, retail, non-profit, museums and higher education.

www.sisterleadersconference.com

www.drkarenhillspruden.com

I Am An Overcomer

When examining the definition of persevere- to continue a course of action even in the face of difficulty or with little or no prospect of success, my mind was drawn to the latter part of the definition, "with little or NO prospect of success." At that point, I begin to question myself, "Is this what people think of me? Should I be insulted? Is this what people expected of me? Are all the negative things that people have spoken over my life true?" Right then I began to look at things from a different perspective.

I was encouraged by a Proverb my father taught me as a child, "Trust in the Lord with all thine heart; and lean not to thy own understanding. In all thine ways acknowledge him, and he shall direct our paths." This is one divine assignment that I will not miss.

I could tell the story that I am the sixth of seven children, of which five did not survive, and I was born blind in my left eye at 2 lbs. 2 oz and not expected to live.

I could tell the story in my childhood that because of my size and my disabilities I was bullied.

I could tell the story that in my high school people gravitated towards me because I was smart and because of what I could do for them not because they had genuine interest in who I was.

I could tell the story that in college I found myself struggling because I was a peculiar person and never really fit in because of my faith.

I could tell the story that in my twenties I became a single mother and endured many years of abuse to keep my family together.

All of these stories I could tell helped to shape me into the person I am today. What's so encouraging about that? Success is defined as the accomplishment of an aim or purpose, the good or the bad outcome of an undertaking. I do not measure my success by the world's standards of obtaining great wealth, vain appearances, or accolades. My purpose in life is to help others see the goodness of the Lord through me, even while facing adversity.

Often times I've been asked "Iva, with all that you're going through how you keep going?" I simply reply, by God's grace. Changing your perspective and the renewing of your mind can literally change the trajectory of your life.

I have enjoyed success in my career as a Certified Medical Assistant, which was far from my life plan to become a doctor. Due to health issues I had to reinvent myself professionally. Until recently I have worked in local government. After 10 years of service, I found myself being confronted daily by oppressive systems that did not align with my faith. In the physical it seemed as though I was obtaining a measure of success but in the spiritual, I was always in warfare.

There was one common denominator in all the negative experiences in my life, I compromised my faith to please others. I have learned that a compromising moral compass is not an option. This decision had repercussions now. Presently, I am once again searching for a new career, juggling finances, and dealing with the cares of life. I am encouraged by the fact that I have grown spiritually and trust that God will see me through. The Proverbs keep me hopeful and pressing.

My name Iva literally means precious or gracious gift from God. In times where I felt down and discouraged my mother always encouraged me and reminded me of who I am Christ. Throughout my life my faith in Jesus Christ has been a driving force that's that has allowed me to persevere even when I thought that I had no more left in me to give. My faith has sustained me.

Now when I examine the definition of persevere, I see it in the spiritual: For every trial and good undertaking, I accomplish GOD'S aim or purpose for my life by means of the Holy Ghost. I face the adversary in accordance with the Word of God demonstrating great resilience. I AM AN OVERCOMER.

Perseverance Principles

1. **Overcome the fear of success.** Fear is the first tool that the enemy uses to distract you from your God given purpose.
2. **Stay focused**. Don't allow circumstances and negative thoughts to overtake you. Have faith that you are hearing God's voice. Trust that God's has given you everything you need to fulfill His assignment.
3. **Walk in your authority.** Use the Word, God's Word to defeat the enemy. Glorify God, bless someone to overcome with your testimony.

Iva Wright is a lifelong caregiver and consultant. Iva has care for family, friends, and strangers for only one purpose: Sharing the love of Jesus Christ. As a consultant she is often called upon to provide resources for those in need with the goal of helping others achieve success. She has enjoyed a career in health care, local government, and event planning. Her most recent endeavor is TuTu's Treasures turning her love for crafting into "Event Devore You'll Love."

How I learned Money Isn't Everything

I finally got that 6-figure MBA salary, complete with bonus plan and stock options. You know what else I got? 70+ hour work weeks. This might have been okay, after all my husband was busy with law school, and we didn't have any kids. What else was I going to do with all my time?

The thing is, the job also came with oodles of criticism. I started to keep count, and it averaged to about five biting comments per day. If you do the math and make a line chart, as we MBA grads like to do, you quickly realize this translates to A LOT of negative feedback each week. There was no balance of positive accolades.

I was excited about this new job and wanted to do well. I was aware that there were many things I needed to learn, including what my boss and everyone else expected of me and how to navigate the new work environment. I knew I would get things wrong and would need someone to help me course-correct. But this wasn't that. This criticism wasn't from a place of care and support. It was a mark of the culture. And it was exhausting.

I managed to persevere through the stings and stabs by finding pockets of light within the organization: a few kind colleagues who knew the power of a smile or joke to change the mood in a room. They became my lifeline. They helped me get through the day, encouraging me to keep my chin up. Somehow, I arrived at my one-year work anniversary!

I'd figured out how to do my job. I could name the company movers and shakers. I knew how to get the boss's ear. And I kind of learned to ignore the toxicity.

Then, it happened. LAYOFFS. My team was on the list. Did I mention my husband was in law school? As in, I was the sole bread winner for our family? But because I'd found a small group of champions at work, something else happened. I was given the opportunity to apply for another job at the company - unlike the other members of my team. I could save my job – *and big fancy salary!*

What do you think I did? I applied for the job. Of course. I got an interview. I crushed the interview. Then I went home and cried.

My body was tired. My spirit was drained. From working all those hours and the onslaught of all that negativity.

But mostly from denying the parts of me that I'd ignored for this job, with its 70-hour work weeks: music, girls' nights, reading, walking the dog, cooking dinner, volunteering, going to church, taking a vacation without checking email.... I had ZERO time for soul-filling endeavors.

What do you think I did next? I got up in the morning and went to work. And then I told the Executive Vice President I wanted a severance package. I walked away from my big 6-figure salary. I walked away from the certainty of a new job. I walked into the unknown. And my eyes shined. I had found the light again. I chose me! I determined the next time I found a job, it would include time for planting flowers, for talking with neighbors, for hiking in the evening.

Years later, I can report that since then on occasion I have made a big fancy salary. But it's never the motivation for doing the work. It becomes one piece of the decision to take that next opportunity. Because you know what's more important? The culture of the place. The encouragement of the people. The opportunity for growth. The chance to cultivate life outside the office. The ability to hold onto the parts that make life worth it.

Perseverance Principles

1. **Your worth is not defined by your paycheck.** You are uniquely made, with talents and values, strengths, and interests. Choose the job that honors all of you, not your bank account.

2. **Shine your light.** Your smile may be just the thing to help a colleague make it through the day. Choose kindness, care, and encouragement over harsh words and criticism.

3. **Listen to your body.** Toxicity takes a toll. Your body will alert you when you've had enough. Choose to walk away towards health, wholeness, and freedom. Choose you.

Ginny Bowen Olson, ICF-certified coach, owns the career strategy firm, Brand Elements Coaching. There, she leverages enthusiasm and careful listening to empower clients to create careers they want. Her specialties include personal and professional branding and executive presence to enable clients, as one described it, to be more confident in their worth. With 20+ years of experience in corporate and nonprofit marketing, she serves as a marketing professor and recently published the book, Strategic Marketing for Nonprofits, to arm nonprofit leaders with tools to solve their marketing challenges. Ginny earned her MBA from Wake Forest University and BA from UVA.

BrandElementsCoaching.com

Coming to America

My journey to America, land of the free, home of the brave included two failed applications for a visitors' visa, but on the third try I was granted the visa for my son and myself. I left my home country of Sierra Leone as a graduate and high school teacher. I intended to stay in America because conditions in Sierra Leone were getting bad and America provided the opportunities I wanted for our family and particularly my two-year-old son. I applied for a social security card on arrival. It was stamped 'not valid for employment' so I transcribed the numbers to a fake wallet social security card, overstayed my visa allowance period, and immediately became an illegal alien as it was called then, an undocumented immigrant, now. Perseverance.

An undocumented immigrant, much against popular thought, can work menial jobs. I came as a graduate, my immigration status meant I had to start from rock bottom. I started working as a nanny and took the GED exam. I missed a couple of questions on purpose so the administrators would not question my intelligence. Next, I took the Certified Nurse Assistant class and started working as a CNA. My son's only identification was his passport, so I put him in a private school where his status was never questioned. Perseverance.

My husband was two years ahead of me arriving in America. He too, as a graduate, needed the GED, worked construction, then respiratory therapy school, and was now working at a local hospital as a respiratory therapist. He came home from work one day complaining of severe neck pain. By the end of the next day, he was on a ventilator completely paralyzed from his neck down. Now, I have a son to take care of and a quadriplegic husband. Perseverance.

I enrolled in nursing school. I had to. Working extra hours to keep our lives together was affecting me. I did not graduate top of my class but became the envy of it when I got hired immediately into the prestigious Intensive Care Unit, courtesy of my extended stay with the staff when my husband was sick. I worked nights, which meant I could care for my family, nap during the day, earn a higher rate of pay, and work at a slower pace. One day, I read a notice that the hospital was filing for and granting legal status to nurses. Bingo! I bravely applied and two years later, my entire family had attained legal status. Perseverance.

My husband died after eight years of being a quadriplegic. My son was fifteen. I had the new challenge of raising a depressed and sad teenager while preparing him for college. I had to set my grief aside, enrolled my son into hospice grief counseling to help deal with the loss of a dad. Whew! He made it into the University of North Carolina at Chapel Hill. Now I can breathe, relax, and focus on myself for a change. Perseverance.

What? Another adventure! I packed up everything, took early retirement and went home to Sierra Leone to open the first dialysis clinic in a country where seven people were dying daily from kidney failure in the capital city, Freetown. I operated the clinic saving lives until I got a call that my son had been put on a medical watch in college and the threat of Ebola in Sierra Leone was becoming widespread. Perseverance.

I withdrew my son from the university a few months short of his graduation and spent time with him overcoming trauma and giving him the love and attention he deserved. My story of perseverance in the land of the free and the home of the brave continues to this day. However, I must conclude by saying, "in all these things I am more than a conqueror through Him who loved us. For I am convinced that neither death nor life, neither angels nor demons, neither the present nor the future, nor any powers, neither height nor depth, nor anything else in all creation, will be able to separate us from the love of God that is in Christ Jesus our Lord." (Romans 8: 37-39) Perseverance.

Perseverance Principles

1. **Humility is the first precursor to perseverance.** Recognizing that you must set aside your pride, take a few steps backward and then purposefully advance into your future.
2. **Hope is the second aspect of perseverance.** The trust and expectation of fulfillment of your desires gives one the strength to proceed bravely and fearlessly with anticipation of a brighter future.
3. **Faith is the final factor in perseverance.** Having the belief that with God first, all things hoped for will come to fruition. Anyone who humbles themselves and puts their hope and their unwavering faith in God will never be put to shame.

Newtona Turner fondly called Tina Turner since marrying Dennis Turner, has been a Registered Nurse for 27 years currently working for Novant Health in the cardio-vascular unit. She holds a bachelor's degree in Home Economics from N'jala University of Sierra Leone, an associate nursing degree from Forsyth Technical Community College, and a master's degree in nursing with an emphasis in Nursing Leadership from Grand Canyon University. Newtona is a mentor, politician, leader, and innovator who opened the first Dialysis Center in Sierra Leone.

Pain and Progress: A Dance of Perseverance

In high school, my life revolved around dance, cheerleading, track and field, show choir, and other extracurricular activities that filled my days with purpose and passion. At 15 years old, everything came to a halt. An injury left me on crutches and in a boot for what became 18 grueling months. A routine injury spiraled into an ordeal that challenged me physically, mentally, and spiritually.

My doctor presented two options: let the injury heal naturally or insert a rod down my leg. The thought of surgery terrified me, and my mother, ever the protector, opted for the natural healing route. We believed that time and faith were on our side, but every passing day felt like an eternity.

The injury wasn't just about the physical pain; it was about the pain of losing everything I loved. I was sidelined, watching, as life moved on without me. My days became a series of exhausting hurdles: maneuvering up three flights of stairs on crutches at home, showering in a chair, and the humiliation of nicknames and jokes from classmates and teachers. The physical challenges were immense, but the emotional toll was just as heavy.

People saw the boot and crutches but didn't see the internal struggle, the frustration, the isolation, and the fear that I might never return to the activities I loved. Every night, I hooked my leg up to a growth simulation machine, hoping it would accelerate the healing process. And every night, in that stillness, I prayed. I prayed for healing, strength, and the ability to endure. My prayer life was my lifeline, the only thing that kept me connected to hope when everything else seemed uncertain. I asked God for physical recovery and guidance. What was I meant to learn through this ordeal?

After 18 months, my leg healed, and I was cleared to return to dance! The relief and gratitude I felt was overwhelming. I threw myself into practice, determined to make up for lost time. During competition, I performed my solo with every ounce of passion and resilience cultivated during my recovery. It placed first, earning the highest score my studio had ever seen at that time. It was a moment of pure triumph, a testament to the power of perseverance and prayer. And just as I began to celebrate my comeback, a familiar pain struck, this time in my right leg. My heart sank as I made my way back to the doctor's office.

The timing couldn't have been worse. My doctor was on vacation. When the same nurse reviewed my X-rays, she disturbed my doctor on vacation due to the shock of her findings. He ordered tests which revealed my body's inability to produce enough calcium. When she entered the room, her shocked expression told me everything I needed to know. I was facing yet another set of stress fractures. My heart sank. How could this be happening again? But even in that moment, I chose not to question God. Instead, I asked Him to reveal what I was meant to learn.

There is a reason for everything, right?

This injury was less severe, and my recovery was much shorter. I returned to my activities with renewed determination. That year, I was named captain of the show choir, won the Judges' Choice Award at competition, and led my almost 50-year-old dance studio to its first-ever Platinum ranking. My A Cappella team took 1st place, and the dances I choreographed for our dance team won at our scholastic competition. The culmination of all this hard work was when I got my first car—a symbol of my independence and resilience. I was ready to finish high school with a bang!

Looking back, I see that my journey was not just about overcoming physical pain but about discovering the strength within myself to face whatever life throws my way. At just 15 years old, I learned that setbacks are not the end but the beginning of something greater. My challenges shaped me into the person I am today—resilient, determined, and grateful for every experience that has made me strong. I carry these lessons, knowing that perseverance isn't just about surviving hardships but thriving because of them.

Perseverance Principles

1. Resilience is built through adversity.
2. Faith and patience can guide you through the toughest challenges.
3. Every setback is an opportunity for growth and self-discovery.

Tishana Jackson is a dynamic entrepreneur and cultural enthusiast, recently earning her master's degree at 22. She owns two small businesses: *Trini Teas*, specializing in handcrafted beverages like boba and iced coffee, and *Inspired by Trinity Grace*, offering digital media services including social media, photography, videography, and graphic design. With 19 years of dance training and a love for travel, Tishana brings creativity, discipline, and a passion for uplifting and coaching those around her.

www.TishanaJackson.com

Judge Me Not

I was a young woman, lost at an early age, struggling to find myself. I fell in love with someone I believed would always be there for me, and at 21, I had my daughter. But when my boyfriend's mother died, he lost himself. He neglected us, and making money became his obsession. Eventually, he left me and our child to fend for ourselves. Things got so bad that we were forced to move. In a moment of desperation, I made an irrational decision: I started dancing in a nightclub. From that point on, I sacrificed everything to provide for my daughter.

For years, I surrounded myself with the wrong people, and the dancing life taught me some of my hardest lessons. I fell in love with another man who wasn't right for me either. He isolated me from my family, and worst of all, from my daughter. Eventually, I left her with my mom and dad and moved in with him. Something inside me knew she shouldn't be where I was going, and that's when my life became a living hell.

Under his roof, I was treated like a servant, not a girlfriend. I was his guinea pig and his money trap—money was all he cared about, not me. He disrespected me daily, cheated with other women, hid me in closets, and physically abused me. Then, I found out I was pregnant. My breaking point came when I went into early labor. For 16 and a half hours, my baby and I both had dangerously low blood pressures, forcing the doctors to perform an emergency C-section. After the birth, I became seriously ill, which plunged me into a deep depression. We were in the hospital for 17 days. My son was born healthy, but mentally, I was in a dark place. That darkness is what ultimately saved my life.

I knew I couldn't return to the abuse. I decided to go back to my mother's home, where I was loved and nurtured by her and my father, and where I could be with my daughter again. I grew up in a good Christian home; my grandmother was a pastor, and I knew better than the choices I was making. My parents never judged me, not even for leaving my daughter with them. I felt I had done what I had to do to protect her from the chaos of my life.

But even after this, I found myself entangled with the same toxic man. I was trapped by a fear I couldn't seem to escape. I needed work and his mother gave me a job, but whatever I earned, he saw it as his own. He manipulated and humiliated me, doing everything in his power to break me. One day, I was struck by severe pain and went to the doctor, where I learned I needed a hysterectomy. Due to complications, I stayed in the hospital for ten more days. I could have died. During that time of deep reflection, I cried and prayed, asking God to forgive me for everything I had done and for any pain I had caused my children.

Today, my relationship with my parents and my children is stronger than ever. I have moved on and cut all ties with the toxic person who once controlled my life. I no longer live in fear or anxiety. Through all my poor choices, I felt God's presence following me, even though I repeatedly pushed Him away. But I realized He never left me.

When I returned home, I learned that my family had prayed for me all along, no matter what.

I thank God for my mom.

I thank God for my dad.

I thank God for my daughter.

I thank God for my son.

I thank God for the friends and family who supported me and helped me persevere. I am now dedicated to growing and loving myself. I fully commit to my family and serving at my church. Today, I lead others to salvation for it is written, "Judge not, and ye shall not be judged: condemn not, and ye shall not be condemned: forgive, and ye shall be forgiven" Luke 6:37 KJV

Perseverance Principles

1. God's Constantly Present. Life's challenges and hardships can be overwhelming, but through it all, God remains a constant presence.

2. Learn from the Past. Our past mistakes do not define us, but they are powerful teachers.

3. Lead by Example. By openly admitting our mistakes and deciding to do better, we can inspire others to avoid similar difficulties.

Vanessa A. Waddington is a devoted woman of faith with a heart full of gratitude and purpose. She is the mother of a 24-year-old daughter flourishing as a teacher. Her 12-year-old son is in the 7th grade, growing into a bright and compassionate young man. Beyond her professional life, she serves at her church, using her life experiences to connect with others and guide them toward their own spiritual growth. Whether she's involved in ministry, mentoring, or simply offering a listening ear, Vanessa's service is driven by her deep faith and a desire to give back to the community that has supported her.

If Not Now When

"We're in the DMV, Bay-beee!" I felt like a real, live Rockstar and was so proud to be leading our team of amazing entrepreneur women who had all made sacrifices to travel together to Maryland for our fall retreat. "Congratulations to each and every one of our brand-new independent sales directors! You've reached the top 2% of our company, and you come from so many different professional and personal backgrounds! Let's see who's in the room! When *"this is you"* please take two steps forward and give us your best seminar wave!"

Category after category was celebrated with almost 100 women stepping back and forth as they grooved with DJ Rocko's tunes, laughing, smiling, and waving at the audience. Then, I heard the MC say "NOT married and NO children" so I stepped up, hyped as usual, and got ready to send my air high-fives to my sister directors reppin' this "young, single & free" category with me, but there I stood, all alone and found myself forcing my signature smile to keep it together. I'll never forget how heart-broken and alone I felt in that moment when all the negative feelings and memories of disappointment came rushing back.

That day I made it my mission to bring my season of singleness to a close. I decided to uproot myself from a community I'd lived in and loved for 14 years for a fresh start. I just wanted what most of the women I loved and admired had - a chance to be married and to be a mom! I kissed a lot of frogs in search of my prince, and I trusted that God was preparing my assigned prince in the wilderness of life too! Hands down he would have to be *special* (interpret that however you like, Sis!), and you know what? He is!

He was there to hold me in his manly "I got you" arms with silence that spoke volumes and love me through my second miscarriage. He was there beside me when all I could do was cry because my stepdad of 32 years passed in my mother's arms sitting on their steps. He was there beside me when I moaned and mourned like never before when my beautiful Mama received her heavenly healing. Oh, all this transpired in the first two years of our marriage.

We have persevered through caregiving, intense grief, and then I made the difficult decision to have a hysterectomy, laying my dream of birthing babies to rest and joined the ranks of a community of women who have experienced the same decision, whom I call my beloved *Hysta Sistas*!

Through my forty plus years of mess I pressed on. There were victories I celebrated along the way. But there were many days I prayed not knowing what God had for me. Oh, and one last thing, the icing on the cake, or should I say delicious mango (that story is for the next book!), I have to share. My husband, the Prince, came with a life-changing blessing; his wide-eyed, amazing daughters who on the first day we met in the little town of Anderson South Carolina said so innocently with hope in their soft voices "are you gonna be our stepmom?" My heart melted instantly.

Now, seven years later those baby girls decided to be courageous and start a new journey living full-time with me and their Dad in OUR home. Decades of comparison, sadness, feeling inadequate and asking, "if not now, when?" have come to a gradual close, and this *bonus* Mama is grateful beyond measure in my 5th decade of life knowing God's timing is perfect.

Perseverance Principles

1. **Trust Him** - Our ways are not God's ways
2. **Give Thanks** - Every experience is shaping and strengthening us for what lies ahead
3. **Keep Believing** – motherhood doesn't always look like we think it should

Taunya Monroe Finley has served in education for over three decades, and now her mission is to encourage women of all ages, but especially her Gen X Sisters, to nurture the Total U! each day. As an esthetician, makeup artist and small business owner in direct sales for over two decades, she embraces this newest season of her journey as a wife and bonus mom! She is creating and celebrating her story like never before in this "50th year of Taunya!"

www.marykay.com/TMonroe1

www.TotalUwithTaun.com

Navigating Life's Warning Signs

My parents served as my initial role models in entrepreneurship. Raised in the inner city of Baltimore City in the 80's, I often mention that I was destined to break generational patterns. Both my parents were teenagers when I was born; my mother, a high school senior, later became a licensed cosmetologist, while my father, a 19-year-old manager at Murray's Steakhouse, concealed his involvement in street activities. The contrast between my parents mirrored the phrase "opposites attract." On my mother's side, the emphasis was on hard work, education, and ethical living, while my father's upbringing was more tumultuous due to exposure to street life, drugs, and alcohol from an early age.

For many years, my identity was intertwined with warning signs. At the age of sixteen, pregnant with my first child, my grandmother handed me a yellow folder she had preserved since I was 3 years old. The folder bore my father's name and the date May 25, 1989, at 6:30 a.m., along with my name, age, and other details. Inside, I found a news article about my father's arrest and some letters he had written to me when I was a child. At 23, my father was a super kingpin sentenced to life without parole, shedding light on my fascination with numbers.

On the other hand, my mother was physically present but mentally absent due to an untreated mental illness, leading to her unexplainable wanderings and my similar tendencies.

Becoming a mother at sixteen was the most challenging period of my life. With no stable parental guidance, no stable home, and lacking coping skills, I navigated my pregnancy while attending Lawrence G. Paquin Middle and High School for pregnant teenagers and mothers, where I could bring my baby to school. My high school major was accounting, and my trade was sewing.

I also benefited from semi-independent living in a program called "Second Chance" for teen moms with one child, offering a furnished apartment, a computer, and a stipend. The rule was to attend school, avoid another pregnancy, and upon graduation, keep the computer and receive priority subsidized housing. I graduated with honors, earned a full scholarship to Baltimore City Community College, and saved money for my future move.

After graduating, I had two more daughters, and when pregnant with my youngest, tragedy struck as my mother was fatally hit by two cars. Prioritizing mental health for my children and myself, we engaged in therapy to navigate life's difficulties. Single motherhood was a tough journey, yet I didn't let circumstances hinder my aspirations. My children witnessed me leveraging my artistic and business management skills to provide for our family. I take pride in being a college graduate, homeowner, and owner of multiple businesses, while mastering coping strategies.

Over time, I've embraced essential qualities that have guided me, with art being my most cherished possession. Recalling articles my father sent me about successful Black female entrepreneurs, I now understand the traits I embody today. My passion for art, poetry, fashion, interior design, and real estate forms the foundation of my business model, serving both as a professional tool and a coping mechanism.

Perseverance Principles

1. Don't let your current situation determine your future, your aspirations, or your attitude. Cultivate inner richness, and it will reflect in your outward demeanor.

2. Leverage your talents to achieve your objectives and make use of the resources within your reach, such as family, friends, and community support.

3. Prioritize mental well-being as a crucial factor in achieving your goals. Developing coping mechanisms is essential for navigating life's obstacles.

Tamara "Ms. TeeKay" Kumoji a native of Baltimore, Maryland, is a versatile artist in the DMV art scene, excelling as a performing poet, storyteller, public speaker, songwriter, fashion designer, and creative director. As a mother of three daughters, she is also a self-published author of "Vibrations of Love" Chapbook and has been writing poetry and short stories for more than 25 years. Additionally, Ms. TeeKay is a founding member of FYBR, LLC, a talent and entertainment company, where she showcases her musical talents and applies her extensive experience and skills in business management.

www.tamshandcrafts.com

What Almost Broke Me Blessed Me

Them:

"You never gonna be anything"

"You are ugly"

"No one wanted you and no one wants you"

"You are the reason why your mother is dead"

Me:

"I am ugly"

"No one wants me"

"I'm fat"

"I am stupid"

I was only one year old, unaware of the tragedy that had occurred in my young life, my mother died in 1974 at the age of thirty-four. I was so innocent and full of life is what my young mind remembers. Life was carefree, it was fun living with my aunt, uncle, cousins, and four siblings in New Jersey. Eventually, that innocence would be taken away and replaced with hurt, pain, and abuse. I learned at an early age that life can present many challenges and, boy, I was not prepared.

71

In 1977, around the age of four, I remember my siblings and I riding in my father's van traveling from New Jersey to North Carolina. We arrived at a large farmhouse that had a huge yard and front porch. I remember seeing cows across the dirt road and large fields. The scene was so different. This seasoned woman walked out wearing a beautiful dress and glasses, for some reason I felt a sense of calmness. She was my grandmother.

My father left headed back to New Jersey while me and my siblings made a new home in Timberlake, North Carolina. Grandma would play an instrumental role in my belief in God and knowing God would get me through some perilous times that were to come. My grandmother was a minister, she found pleasure and joy listening to and playing Mahalia Jackson and The Caravans records which would periodically echo through the house. She took us to church instilling in us a spiritual foundation at an early age.

In 1979, it was decided that my younger brother and I would move to Atlanta, Georgia to live with my other family. My brother was seven and I was six. We were excited about taking our first flight on an airplane. Life in Georgia was grand, giving us the opportunity to be on

Morris Brown College campus daily, admiring all the historic sites, and living in upper middle-class neighborhoods.

Then, life went from grand to hell in a matter of several months. The abuse began and from that point, there was no turning back to the innocence what once was. The beatings were intense; electric cords, lawn mower belts, phone cords, clothing belts, switches, etc. I was constantly accused of doing things that I knew nothing about but would say "I did it" to make the abuse stop. There were numerous beatings that I would see blood on my body and could barely sit down. I remember asking God to help me.

The person we lived with; her daughter would do things so that I got blamed for it. My abuser made me lick dishwasher detergent, drink toilet water, and made me sit on the floor by the bed on a dog leash and chain around my neck daring me to go to sleep throughout the night. I was the reason my mother died which destroyed me mentally. My purity was also taken by a male and female cousin, the sexual abuse scarred me deeply.

In 1984, at twelve years old, we were rescued from our abusers. My brother moved back to New Jersey and I to

North Carolina to live with my grandmother who once again, took me in and assisted me with starting the healing process of overcoming abuse. Her walk with Christ; praying, fasting, attending church, and preaching inspired my walk with Christ. I learned that though life can beat you down, the key is not stay down but brush yourself off, heal, rebuild, and go forth and do what God has called you do.

Here I am, grounded in my own faith, and still standing. I graduated from high school, went to college, and eventually earned my master's. I'm professionally employed, as guess what? A social worker! I listen, have compassion, and show concern for children experiencing trauma. I am an advocate!

Perseverance Principles

1. "Weeping may endure for a night, but joy cometh in the morning." Though I went through, I knew that God had me. Psalms 30:5
2. "And whatever you ask in prayer, you will receive, if you have faith." I prayed for protection while in my situation and prayed to be rescued, it came to pass. Mathew 21:22
3. Heal and Rebuild. Talk about it until you heal and then start rebuilding your life back. Though you won't

forget, don't allow that residue to debilitate and stunt your growth aborting your called life purpose.

Tonja Cates is a Social Worker and Certified Women's Trauma Life Coach living in North Carolina. She has a bachelor's degree in social work from Bennett College and a Master of Psychology from the University of Phoenix. Her background includes 14 years in the HIV/AIDS field where for five of those years she worked under Internal Medicine and Infectious Disease. She provides services to adults and children from all demographics, assisting with resolving various social issues. She provides care and services to include people with substance abuse, the elderly, people with disabilities, the homeless, and those with Intellectual, Developmental, and Mental Disabilities.

Always Follow Your Intuition

Many years ago, I decided to buy a house. At the time, I lived in a beautiful downtown apartment that was conveniently located close to everything and had a view of the skyline. I loved that place! Even though I wasn't fully ready to move, I had a strong nudge to leave and plant roots in a larger place. From there, my journey to find the perfect house began.

I quickly found a realtor and started the process. In hindsight, I didn't choose a realtor that honored my vision and needs. His bottom line was solely to close the deal and that became more evident as the homebuying journey progressed. We looked at places for a couple of months and I finally settled on a new home in an "up and coming" neighborhood. I loved that house, but the neighborhood left a lot to be desired. The developers promised buyers that the community would turn into a trendy place to live in the coming years. I was also told that when this happened, my home would be worth much more than my initial investment. So many times, my intuition told me to pass, but I moved forward anyway.

At the closing table I was given stacks of paperwork to sign. As I was signing, I felt queasy. I also heard a male voice that clearly and strongly said "leave now." I was confused, so I asked the gentleman at the table if anyone had said anything. They told me no and encouraged me to continue signing. Once we were done, I got the keys and left. I wasn't excited. Instead of going to my new house, I stopped and visited a friend that lived by the closing office. Two days later I finally made my way to my new house, and I knew I had made a mistake.

My first day in my new house I went driving around the neighborhood. I had done this many times before, but this time felt different. Within a mile, I got lost and found a new subdivision that checked everything on my wish list. The houses and neighborhood were beautiful, and it was even within my budget. I got out and took a tour of the model home and immediately got sick. With greater urgency I knew I had made a mistake and was clear that this is where I was supposed to live. I went back to my new home, laid down, and vowed to make the best of a "not so great" situation.

Over the next 20 months, I never felt at peace in my home. Additionally, the neighborhood became more unruly, and the promise of change and equity became a distant memory. It felt like every other week there was a new threat or drama that needed to be addressed. At one point, I even had to take my neighbors to court for disruptive behavior. I didn't feel good about coming home. And then one morning, I woke up with clarity. It was time to move!

I decided to rent out my place and move back downtown. I found a rental broker and the journey began. I found the perfect apartment, packed up, and was gone a couple of months later. The broker found the ideal tenants for my house, and I was ready to start my next chapter. For the next 5 years, I rented that house out. Instead of thriving, the neighborhood deteriorated, and it became increasingly difficult to find and keep tenants. At this point, I decided to sell.

I put my house on the market, and it wouldn't sell. Since the neighborhood wasn't thriving, I was encouraged to do a short sale. This means that the bank will take less for what is owed on the house. The bank required the house to be sold in 120 days. If this period wasn't honored, the house would go into foreclosure and the bank would own it. Three potential buyers later, the house sold on day 119. What a blessing! Ignoring my instinct and buying that house created so many challenges in my life. But my biggest takeaway from that situation was to always follow your gut, your intuition.

Perseverance Principles

1. Always follow your intuition. At your deepest level, you know what's right for you.
2. When something doesn't feel right, it usually isn't.
3. It's never too late to correct a mistake. Don't be afraid to pivot and place yourself back on the right path.

Courtney Bell is an ICF Certified Life and Executive Coach, Professor, Trainer and Facilitator, and Certified Reiki Master Practitioner. She has nearly 20 years of experience working with corporate and non-profit teams as well as individual adults and youth to reach their most challenging personal, professional, and business goals and experience sustainable success. Her areas of expertise are Coaching, Training, Leadership Development, and Professional Wellness. Courtney resides in Chicago and is the owner of Courtney Bell Coaches.

www.courtneybellcoaches.com

STAND: When You Have Done All You Can Do!

We have heard "Standing on the Promises of God," but when you are in the trauma, drama, heartbreak, pain, shame, sickness, trial, tribulation or suffering let's be honest, it's easier said than done!

I love God's Word and make declarations over myself, my marriage, my ministry, my children, and my friends often but when the storms blow in you can doubt, you can fret, you can cry, you can complain, you can mourn, you can grieve, you can feel overwhelmed, and wonder what is this all about? I'm doing the best I can, I don't bother anybody, and I try to help everybody, so why am I going through this? Trials can show up at anyone's door but what you have inside your house, like the woman in the bible with her small portion of oil, determines how you sustain and persevere.

Growing up my mother loved God with all her heart and could often be found humming throughout our home. On the other hand, my father was an alcoholic and didn't want to hear anything about God and church. My mother lived a Godly life before her husband and children.

As a child I thought if I tried to do everything right, my father would be so proud and somehow this would stop him from drinking on the weekend, yelling in our house, and releasing upon us the negativity he had stored up all week. I created a "perfectionist spirit" within myself trying to calm my earthly father.

In my adulthood, after I married and moved away, he began attending church and accepted Jesus Christ! My father faithfully attended church until he died of a stroke in 1987.

Now I'm an adult, married, with children and grandchildren and didn't recognize until trials showed up at my house that the perfectionist spirit is ugly. This spirit will cause you to not reach out for help when you are in desperate need; this spirit will cause you to hold yourself captive over circumstances you have no control over; this spirit will have you holding on to past mistakes, past losses, past suffering, and always asking yourself the question, "What did I do?" This spirit will hold you captive by always being kind, loving, compassionate, and patient to everyone else, but not showing that same empathy to yourself!

Then, the unthinkable happened. I received a phone call from HR and the VP of my department that I was going to be displaced from a position I held for almost 10 years. I said thank you with my mouth, but I finally had to admit I was grieving this loss because I didn't get to say goodbye to the people I had worked with for 10 years. My oldest brother of 6 passed only 5 months before this news and they shipped his ashes to the funeral home where I had to do the eulogy.

I realized recently that grieving can show up in a lot of areas and if you don't identify it; anxiety, depression, sadness, loss of energy, loss of sleep, and a feeling of being overwhelmed will follow. I blamed the blues on these symptoms. But then it hit me, I had been working from home for the past 3 years because of COVID-19 receiving less sunlight. The doctor diagnosed me with a Vitamin D deficiency.

Over time I was not feeling well and not improving in my health. One day unexpectedly my friends and my sister showed up at my house. Wait a minute, how did you know I needed you? My perfectionist spirit (Pride) wouldn't allow me to call out and scream – HELP ME!!! My friends came and cried with me, they prayed with me, they cooked for me, and they fixed my hair! Friends aren't anything you should take for granted in life. Thank GOD that HE loves you enough that HE would put true sisters and friends in your life not to judge or condemn you but to help you to STAND, when you don't feel like it! Help you to STAND, when you are crying! Help you to STAND when you have lost the weight and clothes are not fitting as you would like! My friends reminded me that I came running to them when they needed it and helped them to STAND!

Perseverance Principles

1. **STAND.** You are wonderfully and marvelously made by GOD Almighty, stop looking on the outside for validation but accept your inner beauty.
2. **STAND.** On the promises of GOD. You are never alone. Your Creator will never leave you or forsake you, and He wants you to have an abundant life!
3. **STAND.** Ask GOD to help you choose your friends because they will be with you through the good, bad, and the ugly.

Dr. Pamela S. Jackson holds a BA, Business Information Technology from Winston-Salem State University. She received both her Master and Doctorate in Business Administration Leadership from Walden University, Minneapolis, MN. Jackson also has an MDiv and DMin in Preaching from United Cornerstone University. Jackson has 25+ years working in Fortune 500 companies as a technologist specialist. Jackson is a Leadership Trainer, Technologist Specialist, Empowerment Builder, Success Coach, Motivational Speaker, Preacher, and Author. She has authored 8 books and is CEO of her own publishing company, Pureheart Publishing Inc. She is happily married to Bishop Dr. George B. Jackson.

www.drpamelajackson.org

www.pureheartpublishinginc.com

Rising From the Ashes

Life has an incredible way of challenging us, often when we least expect it. For me, this challenge came in the form of heartbreak, a loss that initially felt overwhelming but ultimately paved the way for growth and resilience.

It began in the summer of 2004 when I was head-over-heels in love with Seven. Our relationship was a beautiful adventure filled with laughter, spontaneous road trips, and dreams that seemed destined to unfold. We were inseparable, and I truly believed we were meant to be together forever. But, as life would have it, things took an unexpected turn.

I vividly remember the day it happened. I won't get into what led me to end what I thought would be my forever, but we had inevitably come to a place where a decision had to be made. Although everything in my heart and soul said stay, my head said NO! And so, on that day, "we" became "me"—I felt as though the ground had been pulled out from under me. It was a moment that shattered my world.

In the wake of our breakup, I found myself adrift in an ocean of sadness. The feelings of worthlessness and despair rushed in like a tide, and I often felt trapped in a vortex of emotions I struggled to navigate. I isolated myself, retreating into the comfort of familiar routines cloaked in darkness. For too long, I allowed myself to dwell in the shadows, replaying memories and holding onto what once was.

But as the days turned to weeks, something began to shift within me. One rainy afternoon, while scrolling through social media, I stumbled upon a quote that sparked a glimmer of hope: "You can't start the next chapter of your life if you keep re-reading the last one." Those words resonated and ignited a fire deep inside me. It was time to take action. It was time for a change.

I started small. I picked up a journal and began to pour my thoughts onto the page, allowing my feelings to flow freely. The process became cathartic—not just a release, but a way to reflect and understand myself better. With each entry, I felt the weight of my sadness lift, even if just a little.

Alongside journaling, I threw my emotions into my businesses, Bodied By Ty Aesthetics, HUSLHER Apparel and my ever so fulfilling book club, Chapter Chicks, which delves into real women, real stories, and the triumph over life's stumbles along the way. These were all the things that brought me joy. I rediscovered my love for design, allowing decorating to express what my words couldn't. I reached out to friends I had distanced myself from, and their support became a lifeline. Conversations filled with laughter and genuine connection reminded me of the beauty still present in my life. And GOD, always there, always prodding me and letting me know HE always has my back and always will.

Slowly but surely, I began to heal. I learned to let go of the past and embrace the uncertainty of what lay ahead. I realized that every ending was also a new beginning, and in letting go of what no longer served me, I was creating space for new experiences and opportunities.

As I navigated this transformative journey, I took time for self-reflection. I explored my passions, set new goals, and started to envision the future I wanted. It wasn't just about bouncing back; it was about bouncing forward. I was discovering my strength, resilience, and ability to rise, even in the face of adversity.

Today, as I reflect on that journey, I am grateful for the heartbreak that once felt insurmountable. It taught me invaluable lessons about love, loss, and ultimately, self-love. I stand here, not just as someone who endured heartbreak, but as someone who emerged stronger, more aware, and ready to embrace whatever comes next.

Life is full of twists and turns, but I now know that even in the darkest moments, we possess the power to heal, grow, and soar. Each chapter of our lives, regardless of how challenging, shapes us into who we are meant to become. And for that, I am endlessly thankful.

Perseverance Principles

1. **Embrace Vulnerability** - Acknowledge that experiencing pain and heartbreak is a natural part of life.
2. **Lean on Support Systems** - Recognize the importance of surrounding yourself with a strong support network
3. **Transform Setbacks into Growth Opportunities** - Understand that setbacks are not the end but rather opportunities for personal growth.

Tylicia Jones As a dedicated serial entrepreneur and proud mother of four, I thrive on balancing the demands of family and a fulfilling career. With a full-time career in the life-saving bio-pharmaceutical industry, I am passionate about making a difference in healthcare while driving innovative business ventures. My journey is fueled by the desire to inspire my children and empower those around me to achieve their dreams. I strive to create a positive impact through my work and entrepreneurial pursuits, all while cherishing the precious moments with my family.

www.bodiedbytyaesthetics.com

www.huslherapparel.com

Worthy of More

I work with women owned small businesses. I chose to work with women because I feel we come into business with a unique set of problems. Those problems I understand completely because they plague me too. These issues hold us back from stepping into who we were called to be. Time and time again the biggest issue I see for women business owners is they don't feel they are worthy of success.

I had a client; we will call her Cindy. Cindy came to me because she wanted help with her taxes. She felt that she wasn't deducting all the things she could. After meeting with her and reviewing her finances, I realized that wasn't the problem at all. She wasn't charging enough! Not just slightly but charging so little that she was barely making minimum wage.

When I told her she had to change her prices she cringed. I asked her why did increasing her prices cause her so much anxiety. Cindy said she felt people would leave because they wouldn't want to pay the higher prices.

I worked out all the numbers to show her that even if some clients left, she would be making more money.

She still wasn't convinced so I kept asking questions until I got to the root of the problem. She really didn't feel worthy of charging higher prices.

This right here is the biggest problem holding women back in business. We don't feel we can ask for more money. We feel we must put up with bad clients. We tolerate things that we shouldn't. We don't write the book, start the podcast, ask for more. Why? Because we don't feel worthy. We don't feel worthy of more money. We don't feel we earned success. We don't feel we can turn bad clients away. We were raised that we should be humble and grateful for what we have. We shouldn't seek more because that is greedy. We are to be kind, and we turn that into we must tolerate bad things for the sake of kindness. Women are taught that being aggressive in business is wrong. And worst of all we feel if we love what we do then we shouldn't be paid well for it.

I sat with Cindy for two hours. We talked about why she felt unworthy. She shared her fears, her shame, her anxiety. Every objection she gave me I dissolved. Much of our time was spent with me encouraging her that she was made for more.

Encouraging her that she could ask for more money and her clients wouldn't run away. We even practiced what to say to introduce the price increase, how to handle objections and what to do if she felt the need to discount her services. And at the end of those two hours, she made the brave choice to increase her prices by more than triple.

She said she had never felt so empowered but scared all at once. I understood exactly how she felt because I have felt it so many times myself. I remember the first time I increased my prices. It was terrifying. I told her it would be ok, and she would come out of this stronger and better off than when she started.

I followed up with her a week later and she had indeed raised her prices. She said only one client even questioned it. Most just said, "It's about time." Cindy was so proud of herself. She couldn't believe that she hadn't had the courage to do this sooner.

Where are you settling in life? Where do you want more? It is never too late to get started. Take that first step even if you are scared. Write out all the reasons why you can do this. You will be ok. You are worthy of more.

Perseverance Principles

1. **Recognize Self-Worth** - Most of us don't feel worthy of the things we want. It is a lie we tell ourselves to keep us safe.

2. **Choose Growth Over Safety** - Do you want to play it safe through life or do you want to live a vibrant and fulfilling life? I don't want to play it safe. I did that for too long.

3. **Action is a Choice** - Take the first step. It does get easier. I won't promise you that you will never be afraid again, but you will find that it gets easier each time you step out and do the thing that scares you. Doing nothing is a choice.

Audrey Blackburn is the President and Founder of Blackburn Consulting, Accounting and Tax, an accounting and business consulting firm that serves women owned businesses and women led nonprofit organizations. The focus is providing accounting, consulting and advisory services to these leaders and organizations to move them from a place of scarcity to one of abundance. Prior to founding Blackburn Consulting, Accounting and Tax in 2015, Audrey held many financial positions over her 30+ years of experience. She holds a bachelor's in business from UOP and a Master of Accountancy from Gardner-Webb University.

www.blackburnconsultingnc.com

Tea Party

The walls of my nice 3 bedroom, two full baths, apartment had begun to close in. I wanted a house. Not just for additional space. My parents were unwed teens who emphasized the point of homeownership. It allowed them to own rental property and build wealth.

The bank sent me one of those "you-could-be-pre-approved-for-$$$ for a home loan" letters! Well by about the 3rd or 4th notice I said, I'm going to take you on your word. I got in my car, drove to the bank, set the notice on the banker's desk and said, "Here you go, I'm ready."

He asked some questions, ran some numbers and gave me a pre-qualified letter for way more house than I wanted. I was overjoyed! I walked out of his office, to my car, sat down, and cried! I made my way upstairs to my 3rd floor apartment with haste to get on Realtor.com to find my new home.

After selecting many, and being shown several, Tracy, my realtor and I found my home. It was a fixer-upper built in the 70's where the previous owner added many modern-day amenities including a laundry room, screened in porch, and a two-car garage. What sealed the deal was the huge den-to-kitchen-dining-area that could seat 20+ people comfortably in one space for a tea party, cucumber sandwiches and all!

I worked a discount on the property because much of it was in bad shape. I put down my due diligence, (the non-refundable-I'm-serious-about-buying-this-house-money), and waited for further instructions.

Next, I went back to the bank to work up the loan papers. I walk into the office beaming with excitement, Jon, the banker asked some questions, ran some numbers, and said, "Your loan is denied."

Wait—

What?

You gave me a pre-qualification letter stating I qualified for twice the amount of the house I selected. "Yes, but that letter is not a pre-approval, just a pre-qualification." After his explanation of the difference, I walked out of his office, to my car, sat down, and cried! I made my way upstairs to my 3rd floor apartment with haste, to get on the internet to find a new home loan.

I made calls to my circle of family and friends in banking or real estate for advice. In about a week I got another one of those "you-could-be-pre-approved-for-$$$ for a home loan!" This time it's $50,000 more than the last one.

I got in my car, drove to the bank, and set the notice on the banker's desk and said, "Here you go. This is your institution. You keep sending these unsolicited notices to me. This one is for more than the last. Honor your word. That's all I want is for you to honor your word!"

The hold up was not my credit score, income, or payment history, it was a large amount of student loan debt, plus my primary and largest source of income comes from entrepreneurship in a system that makes it more difficult for a Black Woman Entrepreneur to secure funding. (I'm not here to debate this with you.)

So, Jon, advocated for me. I know he did. How? I just know. Jon, is a devoted husband and father. He and his wife love the outdoors, and over the years we talked many times about life, culture, family, and green leafy plants.

In my home, within the first year I hosted a homeless mother and her 4 children abandoned by a spouse, a friend who went through a tumultuous divorce and needed rest and slept for 3 days, a woman who was depressed and suicidal who is now excited about living again, and I have made countless meals for friends, family and neighbors, had people come and stay who just needed rest from life and I provided a hot meal, cup of tea, or a clean warm bed to revive and reset, people meet here for bible study and fellowship, and tea parties! It's been less than 3 years.

I did all of these things when I lived in an apartment. I didn't wait for the house. My faithfulness over the apartment opened the door to the house. The enemy is defeated, and God is always glorified. The next house will be bigger in size and purpose.

Perseverance Principles

1. **Be Grateful** – Gratitude over your current situation and your current blessings—opens doors to greater opportunities.
2. **Be Relational** – Transactional living—this for that— requires you to always have something to give. Relational living requires you to be kind towards other humans.
3. **Be Persistent** – Pursue your goals despite setbacks or rejections. Stay determined and push forward even when things don't go as planned.

Dr. *Timogi*

About the Curator

"I lead individuals and organizations from Elusive to Empowered."

Dr. Timogi is a Master Facilitator and Executive Trainer with extensive experience in corporate, nonprofit, and higher education leadership.

She is the founder of Create & Facilitate, a North Carolina HUB Certified Customized Training Solutions Agency, specializing in personal and professional development, workshops, leadership retreat facilitation, and employee mediation.

As an international keynote speaker, Dr. Timogi has inspired and trained diverse audiences, ranging from correctional facilities to prestigious institutions like Harvard. She is also the author of 15 books and numerous customized training programs, demonstrating her commitment to empowering individuals and organizations worldwide.

Book Dr. Timogi Today!

Customized Training Solutions

Keynote Speeches

Panel Discussions and Panel Moderator

Lectures

Individual and Group Coaching

Conferences

Employee Training and Development

Commencements

Workplace Conflict Mediation

Retreats

CONTACT INFORMATION

PO Box 334

Lexington, NC 27293

www.DrTimogi.com

www.CreateAndFacilitate.com

Made in the USA
Columbia, SC
28 October 2024

45174910R00065